THE MONO BOX PRESENTS **PLAYSTART**

The Mono Box presents
PLAYSTART

Short plays from new voices

OBERON BOOKS
LONDON

WWW.OBERONBOOKS.COM

First published in 2018 by Oberon Books Ltd
521 Caledonian Road, London N7 9RH
Tel: +44 (0) 20 7607 3637 / Fax: +44 (0) 20 7607 3629
e-mail: info@oberonbooks.com
www.oberonbooks.com

PB ISBN: 9781786827081
E ISBN: 9781786827074

Cover photo by Helen Murray / Arenapal

Printed and bound by 4EDGE Limited, Hockley, Essex, UK.
eBook conversion by CPI Group (UK) Ltd, Croydon, CR0 4YY.

10 9 8 7 6 5 4 3 2 1

Contents

Foreword

Hello. My name is Susan Wokoma and I am an actor SLASH writer.

Now I dunno about you but it definitely feels like the entertainment industry is positively (in both senses) swelling with us pesky multi-hyphenates, hyphenating around. Nothing is more indicative as the fact that all the writers selected as part of this year's PLAYSTART initiative are all, like me, performer slash writers.

Why is this the case? Is it coincidence? Actors are meant to be the ones sitting by the phone, dependant on other people giving them the thumbs up to do some acting, right? Well not anymore and thank goodness for that I say. What we are seeing are actors utilising that unique fearless, instinctive creativity that we have to tell our own stories. To not wait by the phone. To create the characters we so crave to see on our stages and screens. It took me ages to convince myself that the years and years of experience reading and dissecting scripts meant something. That all those hours of dramaturgical investigation could perhaps stand me in good stead in creating my own narratives. It is therefore truly thrilling that The Mono Box – a company I am so proud to be a patron of – have found these five fellow, brilliant multi-hyphenates and put them in this play text for you to enjoy. It is no coincidence – in my opinion – that this is the case as The Mono Box have been providing a safe fun space for creatives to mine playtexts, as I have done, for years.

Having attended PLAYSTART last year, I was completely swept away by how much the room was fizzing with creativity. It felt like the early days of acting and collaborating and devising, when there wasn't that sometimes ugly constricting pressure to 'put on the finished product'. It felt organic. I could really hear the writers' voices. It was FUN, contagious and I am utterly unsurprised that most of the plays from that year have been picked up for development by theatres such as The Yard, The King's Head and The Kiln.

There is something magical about the written printed word. It travels so far and so wide and ends up being read by thousands of people. Too many times I have seen work-in-progress pieces performed and wished there was a way to read what brilliance I had just witnessed. Or all too frequently I'll be asked for monologue or duologue suggestions for drama school and I'll remember that great scene I-saw-in-that-thing, unable to get my hands on the work itself to pass. So this year it is such a thrill to be able to write the foreword in *'The Mono Box presents PLAYSTART – short plays from new voices'* and to have Oberon brilliantly and cleverly publish it because – guess what? These chosen five writers are now PUBLISHED writers. I won't have to go on a mission to track down their work and pass it on. It will be here. Published. For so many to enjoy. It will mean something – not just personally – to these writers but professionally. Oberon are saying 'we want to support new talent and we believe in them enough to publish their work'. That is invaluable and I hope that this great faith in these new voices will urge theatres to not overlook these actor SLASH writers. You want new diverse talent? Well here they are.

Now, I'm going to go away and continue hyphenating somewhere whilst you get stuck in to some exciting new writing talent. It's important to cultivate and nurture such promise. Let's keep curious and collaborating and celebrating wonderful work.

Susan Wokoma

An Intro to Playstart

Each play in this inaugural collection is fifteen minutes long. Like other 'shorts' mediums, short plays offer a window into a new voice and the narrative drives straight to the core of what the writer is trying to say.

As you read through the book, notice how the performance springs to life because of the writer's deep understanding of how to support the actors that are going to realise their words. This is invaluable. And then there are the stories that they are choosing to tell: Graeme's absurdist comedy about class has me laughing and screaming in the same breath. Sid's lyrical piece about the complexity of a father and daughter relationship moves me to tears. Then there's the gentle nuance taken in Aisling's play which is an incredibly well observed take on a seemingly mundane situations. Roberta's fast paced play about challenges our relationship to the make-up industry and Charles's two-hander is a sharp-twisting tale of survival.

I resonate with the variety of these stories because I am a storyteller. In the world that we currently find ourselves in we must keep finding the vehicles for a range of existences and experiences to take the platform and share the space. Many stories are still not being told, but PLAYSTART has uncovered five excellent ones from names that I think we will be hearing from for a long while yet.

Graeme Brookes, Charles Entsie, Roberta Livingston, Sid Sagar, Aisling Towl.

Remember their names.

Enjoy their stories.

PLAYSTART is just the beginning.

Joan Iyiola

A Brief History of The Mono Box

It's 2006 and two actors, Joan and I, Polly, met in rehearsal room at the National Youth Theatre. A British Nigerian and a girl from Watford, we struck up a friendship in a cast of mainly boys and discussed how in the future we would take over the world. Neither of us knew exactly how we would do this, but we both enjoyed theatre and found each other incredibly funny so that was a good start.

Three years later, after doing the things our parents wanted us to do at University, Joan was doing a post grad in Acting at Bristol Old Vic Theatre School, and I was based in London at Royal Central School for Speech and Drama doing a Movement MA. But when we graduated we grappled with what came next. Support networks for young actors and theatre-makers were fast disappearing to funding struggles and we noticed an air of competition amongst our peers. The education system had taught actors about end goals and people became protective about what they knew. Some theatres offered us the chance to listen to established actors talk onstage about their lives, but none of them knew what it was like to be hunting for experience like us. Workshops were expensive and inaccessible; there were few places to go to share knowledge.

Throughout it all though we were a team; we would be a support network for each other. Joan shared her knowledge of Shakespeare with me for an upcoming interview and I suggested plays for Joan to perform for a showcase. We read plays, saw theatre together and talked about our next steps, and soon we invited other people into the conversation.

We started approaching the industry professionals we admired. We asked them what play they would recommend actors in our position to read and, boldly, whether they'd consider sending a copy to us. The letters went out and we waited. And waited…

And then, the first batch of plays arrived: a collection of short plays from Caryl Churchill, a copy of the play Dame Judi Dench felt she'd missed the chance to be in, the first play Cillian Murphy was in in the West End and David Tennant's favourite text. Surely, and steadily more plays came through the door, each inscribed by their donor with personal insight and advice ready for whoever reads it. We were on to something. The plays kept coming. The Mono Box was born.

We started sharing the plays at Speech Surgeries, a monthly event to provide access to the collection and find their audition speeches. People came, happy to put an end to stealing time on bookshop floors and happy to share conversations about writing, acting and the obstacles they were facing to our panels of professionals who were also negotiating the industry themselves.

Speech Surgeries were everything we had wanted them to be. The atmosphere fizzed and people felt inspired to keep going. As we negotiated the industry for ourselves, we started to break down and demystify it for other people.

Speech Surgeries are still our flagship event but over the last five years The Mono Box developed wider than we could have ever imagined. Over the last five years, The Mono Box has welcomed over 4,000 actors through its doors and had a strong, long-lasting impact. By listening to the anxieties and obstacles people were encountering outside of drama school auditions, we are able to build a workshop programme tailored to what actors felt they were not getting elsewhere. We invite our peers and colleagues from Olivier-winning directors, award winning writers and casting directors to facilitate sessions, so The Mono Box's output is always feeding what is going on in the industry right now.

As a result of securing our own permanent space this year, our current workshop programme is more diverse than ever; from offering participants the opportunity to work with playwrights to sessions with directors analysing classical text; from trying African dialects to embracing movement and clowning, devising and film-making, The Mono Box reflects what the industry is demanding from actors and provides affordable access to the skills they need.

The Mono Box has grown into a community of emerging, working and enduring artists and PLAYSTART has been a natural extension of that. In learning that many actors were secretly writing behind closed doors tied with our mission to encourage and enable professional development, PLAYSTART was created to provide an opportunity for new writers to share their work. We team each new writer with an established playwright to mentor them through the process, select directors and help these teams cast the plays from our pool of actors. The companies are then provided access to free workshops and talks, rehearsal space and mentorship from other Mono Box associates before a showcase to an invited industry and public audience.

Of last year's cohort, all of the plays supported by The Mono Box went on to have a further life at other theatres, and the creative partnerships have sustained. The interest in PLAYSTART this year was extraordinary; with over 700 applications for only twenty-six places we know that The Mono Box is attracting new voices and delivering unique opportunities for young people to create away from conventional training. The people involved this year are a mix-tape of talents; a reminder to us all that we don't need to do one thing for the rest of our lives. Authentic creativity comes from trying new things.

PLAYSTART encapsulates what makes The Mono Box special. To see collaboration happen in the purest form and encourage young people to take charge of making the work they want to make rather than what is offered to them is a real thrill. Over the past five years our greatest moments have been when we see actors sharing speeches with each other with the knowledge it may suit their new friend more than them. We love when we see people take a workshop friendship and turn it into a show, and we are touched when we see people returning to our sessions after finishing a drama school course they got onto with our help. In providing opportunities to create a dialogue between the professional world and those who are emerging into it, The Mono Box participants have earned places at accredited drama schools, booked jobs and had the confidence to keep going when the odds haven't swung in their favour: exactly what we set out to do.

Now, with over 5,000 people applying for drama school each year and only a few hundred places to fill, who supports those who don't get a place? Where can graduated actors go to keep learning? Who can offer all actors an alternative training and combined emotional support?

The answer is The Mono Box.

And you are welcome any time.

Polly Bennett

Biographies

Graeme Brookes

Graeme is an actor and writer. Graeme has been acting on stage and screen for over thirteen years, working with the Royal Shakespeare Company as well as performing across the UK, Europe & New York. As a writer, Graeme wrote the short film *OneinFive* about a male victim of domestic abuse, which won multiple awards at the BAFTA qualifying: KinoFilm festival and was shortlisted at many others including Palm Springs International Film Festival.

Charles Entsie

Charles Entsie is an Actor/Writer. He began writing after continuously being faced with the difficulty of finding pieces that somewhat depicted the atmosphere he grew up in. He particularly enjoys raw and uncensored work – and most recently appeared at The Bunker Theatre apart of The Wo Lab Actor-Writer Showcase where he performed his piece *Bossman.*

Roberta Livingston

Roberta Livingston is an actor and writer from East London. She co-wrote *Bite Your Tongue* for Talawa Young People's Theatre in 2017. Previous acting credits include *The Village* at Theatre Royal Stratford East. *La Merde* is a satirical play about the growing beast that is the YouTube beauty world. This play would be nothing without the amazing The Mono Box team (Polly, Joan & Alison I owe you big time), Lisa Carroll, Fiona Kingwill, Modupe Salu, Alex Marlow, Laura Joy Pieters, Gabrielle Macpherson and my gorgeous mother Brenda.

Sid Sagar

Sid is an actor and writer based in London. He lived abroad before moving to England at the age of eight. He read History at the University of Bristol. On stage, he has performed at Shakespeare's Globe, with the Royal Shakespeare Company, and in an Olivier-nominated play at the Tricycle. On screen, he has worked on several projects for the BBC and ITV, and in films directed by Kenneth Branagh and Steven Spielberg. His short plays have been produced at the Southwark Playhouse, Theatre503, and by Tamasha. *Papa* is his first published play.

Aisling Towl

Aisling Towl is a writer and actor from London. She trained at The BRIT School and Mountview and is currently studying History at Goldsmiths. As a poet she has performed across London and the UK, at venues such as The Lyric Hammersmith, Brainchild Festival and Roundhouse, and is part of The Writing Room 2018 at Apples and Snakes. She is a dedicated napper, Frida Kahlo worshipper and a lover of all types of bread. *Godfrey* is her first play.

Alison Holder, Producer

Alison is an independent producer, currently an English Touring Theatre Forge Associate and Company Producer for Helen Chadwick Song Theatre. Previously she was Producing Coordinator at the Bush Theatre.

Productions include: *Future Bodies* by RashDash/ HOME/ Unlimited Theatre (HOME and UK tour); *Truth* by Helen Chadwick and Steven Hoggett (Birmingham Rep, Southbank Centre and UK tour); *Becoming* by Ayo-Dele Edwards (Stratford Circus Arts Centre); *Booby's Bay* by Henry Darke (Finborough Theatre / Wardrobe Theatre, Porthcothan Cornwall); *How It Ended* by Hannah Khalil (Bush Theatre).

Through Alison's audio platform LunAH Productions audio includes: *Barnardo's Black History* and *Single* (BBCR4).

The Mono Box Co-Founders

Polly Bennett

Polly Bennett is a Movement Director and Choreographer working in the broadest applications of movement both nationally and internationally. She holds an MA in Movement from the Royal Central School of Speech and Drama and is Associate Movement Practitioner at the Royal Shakespeare Company. **Theatre credits include:** *The Lehman Trilogy* (National Theatre), *The Village* (Stratford East), *Maydays* (RSC), *The Great Wave* (National Theatre), *Circle, Mirror Transformation* (HOME), *People, Places and Things* (National, West End and off-Broadway), *Salome* (RSC), *A Streetcar Named Desire* (Royal Exchange), *Travesties* (Menier Chocolate Factory, West End), *A Midsummer Night's Dream* (RSC), *Doctor Faustus* (Duke of York's), *The Maids* (Trafalgar Studios), *Yen* (Royal Court), *Three Days in the Country, Nut* (National Theatre), *Hang* (Royal Court). **Film:** *Bohemian Rhapsody, The Little Stranger, Stan & Ollie.* **TV:** *The Crown* (Series 3), *Killing Eve* (BBC America), *Urban Myths* (Sky Arts), Gareth Malone's Best of British (BBC One.) She was Assistant Movement Director on the London 2012 Olympic Opening Ceremony and Mass Cast Choreographer on the 2014 Sochi Winter Olympics and Paralympic Opening Ceremonies. She is a performance mentor for choirs and singers.

Joan Iyiola

Joan trained at the Bristol Old Vic Theatre School, Cambridge University, Complicite and The National Youth Theatre. **Theatre credits include**: *The Duchess of Malfi* (RSC), *Boudica* (Shakespeare's Globe), *They Drink it in the Congo* (Almeida Theatre) *Omeros,* (Shakespeare's Globe & St Lucia Transfer), *The Convert, Eclipsed, The Rise and Shine of Comrade Fiasco* (Gate Theatre); *You're so Relevant, A Season in the Congo* (Young Vic); *A Midsummer Night's Dream, The White Devil, Arden of Faversham, The Roaring Girl, Boris Godunov, The Orphan of Zhao, A Life of*

Galileo (The Royal Shakespeare Company); *Toilet* (Southwark Playhouse); *Holiday* (Bush Theatre); *The 24 Hour Plays, Sex Toys, His Spirits Hear Me* (The Old Vic). **TV includes:** *Black Earth Rising* (BBC/Netflix), *Enterprice* (BBC), *New Blood* (BBC One), *Yonderland* (Sky) **Film includes:** *Denial, The Dead Sea, Words, Show Dogs.*

Acknowledgements

Thanks to our producer Alison Holder, our playwright mentors Tristan Bernays, Lisa Carroll, Hannah Khalil, Arinzé Kene and Rory Mullarkey, our patrons Sir Derek Jacobi, Susan Wokoma, James Norton, Vanessa Kirby, Annie Tyson, Joseph Marcell and Danny Kirrane, our board Joe Iyiola-Bell, Catriona Guthrie, Fiona English, Alfred Bridi, Hannah Osborne, Pippa Hill at RSC, Zoe Ford Burnett, Andy Whyment, Helena Clark at Casarotto, Nic Wass at RSC, Ingrid Mackinnon at MoveSpace, Ned Bennett, David Edgar, Helen Murray and to our incredible team of volunteers who make all of the Mono Box magic happen.

First performed at The Biscuit Factory, London, Wednesday 28th November 2018 with the following cast:

The Interview
Directed by Emma Baggott
INTERVIEWER 1 Mariah Louca
INTERVIEWER 2 Benjamin Salmon
INTERVIEWER 3 Phoebe Naughton
JANE Anna Ash Mackay

NSA
Directed by Imogen Wyatt Corner
BOY Aaron Cyrus Ward
MAN Martin Edwards

La Merde
Directed by Fiona Kingwill
MACKENZIE Laura Joy Pieters
DEX Alex Marlow
CHRISSY Modupe Salu
ALLEGRA Gabrielle Macpherson

Papa
Directed by Samantha Hardie
RAVI Selva Rasalingam
LAYLA Sofia Cala

Godfrey
Directed by Roberta Zuric
CARYS Harriet Leitch
JASON Sammy Attalah
SIMONE Lauren La Rocque
GODFREY Alex Kerr

THE INTERVIEW

by Graeme Brookes

Writer's Notes

The characters of the 'Interviewers' upon their initial entrance and the beginning of the interview are to be played naturalistically. As the interview progresses, their behaviour, use of the specific props and general demeanour will become more exaggerated, unrealistic and grotesque.

Beside the initial first line of the character, the majority of the lines of the interviewers are not written colloquially (there are the odd exceptions) even though they're to be performed with a strong regional accent. When performed – the actors should approach and use the text and make it fit colloquially. The regionality of the accents do NOT have to be fixed to the ones named in this script.

The actress (Anna Ash Mackay) playing Jane in the first production of 'The Interview' is Scottish – therefore there was an additional line that Jane doesn't own a St George's Flag due to her being 'Scottish'. This line can be removed to accommodate the regionality of the actor playing the role in the future.

The stage is in darkness. A spotlight rises on a chair that is down stage. The only light. It fades down as a wide light fades up to reveal a long meeting table with three chairs set behind it, there is a clothes rail behind each chair. Three characters walk in.

Interviewer 1 – Female. Power Suit. Strong colour. Business. RP.

Interviewer 2 – Male. Polo Shirt & Tied Jumper, Chino Shorts. RP.

Interviewer 3 – Female. Artistic & Eclectic image. RP.

They carry a pull along case, a briefcase and a Fjallraven Kanken bag respectively. They are all carrying garment holders. They don't speak upon entry. In a very formal way they approach the chairs at the table, hang their garment holders on the clothes rail and place their bags on the table.

1:	Shall we?
2:	For sure.
3	Do we have everything?
1	I do.
2:	I do.
3	Then let's.

'Time to say Goodbye' (Bocelli & Brightman) plays. They take in the music and after a while begin to take their clothes off. They do this in a controlled manner until they're in their undergarments. These are high end, matching and branded under garments. They walk together towards their garment holders and unzip them. They take out their costumes.

Interviewer 1 – A pink stained starry onesie.
Interviewer 2 – Old worn Tracksuit bottoms, a stained vest
Interviewer 3 – Jeggings and low-cut vest with a different coloured bra.

Once changed, they return to their bags collectively. Each bag contains specific items.

Interviewer 1 – Two large bags with McDonalds food & drink inside.
Interviewer 2 – A large collection of 'Vape Sticks'.
Interviewer 3 – Large collection of Accessorise style make-up.

They arrange these items very specifically to make sure that it won't impede them around the table, it's very specific and clearly for show. Once completed they all sit down. The music stops.

1:            Are we ready?

2:            Yes.

3:            Almost *(loosening the lids of the numerous items in front of her).*

2:            Wait *(quickly tests his placed vape sticks).* I'm ready.

1:            Prepare.

They all sit very straight backed. Very formal. As if they're preparing for the Queen.

BLACKOUT

Spotlight on the chair in the room. As JANE sits. Once seated, the lights return

JANE: Hello, I'm Jane.

From this point, the accents of the interviewers change as do their physical mannerisms and characteristics.

Interviewer 1 – now speaks in a Yorkshire accent.
Interviewer 2 – now speaks in a Birmingham accent.
Interviewer 3 – now speaks in an Essex/London accent.

3:            Hiya babes!

2:	Ow am ya bab?
1:	Eh up cock!
3:	Jane, it's a pleasure to meet you.
1:	Thank you for your application to join us here at the 'Committee of Working-Class advocates of Culture', also known as … 'Cow-Cac'.
2:	We love an acronym.
1:	We are the premier organisation in meeting the needs of the working classes. We are here to provide you with support both physically, emotionally, monetarily …
3:	That means giving you money.
2:	Not for booze and bingo!
1:	No. Cow-Cac are here to give your people the leg up you so thoroughly deserve and are constantly denied by the oppressive society that we currently reside in. Cow-Cac put the …
2 & 3:	POW!
1:	Into Empowerment!
2:	Your application states that you want to join us at Cow-Cac?
3:	To be Cow-Cac?
1:	When it comes to life satisfaction, you can't get better than getting deep into Cow-Cac. And trust us when we tell you – we are full of Cow-Cac.

2:	Full of it.
3:	Brimming with it.
1:	We are a non-violent organisation however we do fight …
3:	Oh we fight.
2:	We fight hard.
1:	We fight for the great unwashed.
2:	That's yow.
1:	We support the working class. We want to look like *you*.
2:	Yow.
3:	Talk like *you*.
2:	Yow.
1:	Act like *you*.
2:	Yow. We am yow.
JANE:	What sorry?
2:	*(returns to initial accent)* We are you.
1:	Jane, if you own the lifeboats, you own the working class. And we own those lifeboats and we want to help you get on board Jane.
3:	Consider us life guards.
2:	We are lifeguards.
1:	Some people stand in the darkness, afraid to step into the light. Some people need to help somebody when the edge of surrenders in sight.

2 & 3:	*sing* Don't you worry, it's gonna be alright.
1:	Cause we're always ready and we won't let you out of our sight.
3:	Now Jane, we've been told that the questions are similar to the ones asked when you sign on, so they should be familiar.
1:	They are essentially to determine whether you can be Cow-Cac. When it comes to talking for us, you need to be full of Cow-Cac. We are.
2:	Full!
3:	We need you to represent the working classes.
2:	You have to be 'them' …
JANE:	That'll be easy for me.
1:	Why?
JANE:	I am one of them.
2:	We'll be the judge of that.
JANE:	Okay, but I am from a working …
3:	We'll be the judge of that.
2:	And we are good judges.
3:	Not as good as Judge Judy.
2:	But much better than Judge Rinder.
1:	Do you understand everything we've said?
JANE:	Yes.
1:	Good. Then we'll begin.

1 opens a burger, 2 begins vaping, 3 prepares the make-up items and starts adding make-up.

1:	Do you still blame Thatcher?

Beat.

2:	Do you live on Facebook?
3:	Do you share posts from the English Defence League?
JANE:	No.
2:	Tommy Robinson?
JANE:	Definitely not!
1:	Do you share posts demanding to know why you can't publicly display your St George's flag?
JANE:	No.
3:	Scared of looking like a racist?
JANE:	No.
2:	Would you proudly display your St George's Flag?
JANE:	Yes.
3:	Sure you aren't a racist?
JANE:	No. Yes!
1:	Why don't you want to proudly display your St George's Flag?
JANE:	I don't own one.
1:	Why not?

JANE:	I'm Scottish.
2 & 3:	*(Inhale of shock.)*
1:	Okay – let's not get drawn into this. What does your Dad do?
3:	Does he refuse to read a paper that requires you to fold it?
2:	Bad publications.
1:	Were your only holidays from the tokens you got from the Sun?
3:	Just awful.
1:	What's your last name?
JANE:	Shade
3:	Interesting.
1:	Can we start to rattle through these now?
2:	Yes.
3:	Definitely.
1:	Sorry Jane.
2:	Jane Shade.
1:	Sorry Mrs Shade. Or is it Miss?
3:	She could be a Ms.
2:	They do divorce early.
3:	Because they marry early.
1:	Because they breed early.
JANE:	It's Miss.

3:	Good. They never work.
2:	Talking about weddings …
1:	Do you make sure you're never the first person to go up to the buffet at a wedding reception?
2 & 3:	*(Scream.)*
1:	Do you ever use the plastic cutlery?
2:	Why are your wedding buffets like a corridor from Scooby Doo?
3:	Sandwiches.
2:	Chicken leg.
1:	Vol-au-vents.
3:	Pickled Onions.
2:	Prawn Ring.
1:	Pineapple & Cheese.
3:	Sandwiches.
2:	Chicken leg.
1:	Vol-au-vents.
3:	Pickled Onions.
2:	Prawn Ring.
1:	Pineapple & Cheese.
3:	Sandwiches.
2:	Chicken leg.
1:	Vol-au-vents.

3:	Pickled Onions.
2:	Prawn Ring.
1:	Pineapple & Cheese.
2:	Do you wipe your dirty fingers on your socks?
3:	Do you know all the dance moves to Whigfield's Saturday night?
1:	Where does the Music Man come from?
3:	Jane?
2:	Jane Shade?
JANE:	Sorry, who?
1:	The music man.
JANE:	I'm sorry?
1:	*(Almost singing.)* I am the music man, I come from …

Beat.

2 & 3:	… . Down your way.
1:	What can you play?
2:	I play the … .

Beat.

1:	What does he play?
3:	Jane?
2:	Jane Shade?
JANE:	I don't know.

1:	I play the Piano.
2 & 3:	Pi-Pi-Piano, Piano, Piano *(Singing whilst doing the actions.)*
1:	Or … I play the Trombone.
2 & 3:	Umpa-Umpa-Um pa pa, Um pa pa, Um pa pa *(singing whilst doing the actions).*
1:	Or … I play the Bagpipes.

They all stand and jig whilst singing 'Scotland the Brave'. After the first verse, they laugh and almost celebrate.

1:	Okay. I think we've lost you haven't we Jane?
JANE:	Yes.
2:	Don't you know the Music Man?
JANE:	No, I've never heard of him.
3:	Or the song?
JANE:	No, haven't heard of it either.
1:	Shaddauppayaface?
JANE:	I'm sorry, I …
2 & 3:	Hmmmmm.

Beat.

1:	How do you eat a Crème Egg?
3:	Have you ever done a small food shop in Poundland?
JANE:	Yes
2:	Hmmmmmmmmm.

3:	Don't mind all the foreign writing?
JANE:	No
3:	Don't mind the foreigners then?
JANE:	No. I grew up in a multicultural area.

Beat.

1:	Do you eat Avocado?
2:	Hummus?
3:	Quinoa?
2:	Wholemeal Pasta?
JANE:	Yes, Yes, No, No.
1:	What's your favourite take away?
2:	Indian?
3:	Korma? Tikka Masala?
2:	Chinese?
3:	Chicken Sweet and Sour? Crispy Shredded Beef?
JANE:	I prefer a chippy tea to be honest.
1:	A what?
3:	Chippy?
2:	Is that like Chipper?
1:	To be cheerful?
JANE:	No, Chippy as in 'a Chip Shop'. I prefer Fish and Chips. With mushy peas.
2:	Wow.

1:	Not very multi-cultural with your food.
3:	Sure you aren't a little bit racist?
JANE:	No!
3:	Sorry.
1:	Do you trust people who eat Olives?
2:	Did you know that Cottage Cheese is made in Cottages in the Cotswolds?
JANE:	I didn't.
2:	Did you know a Haggis is a small Scottish Hedgehog that lays Scotch Eggs?
JANE:	No it isn't.

Beat.

1:	Back to the interview please.
3:	Jane.
2:	Jane Shade.
1:	Do you ask for Pinot Grigo *(Gre-Jeo)* or Pinot Grigo *(Grig-Eo)*?
3:	When eating – Do you abide to the five second rule?
2:	Did you make your own tip tops?
1:	Ice Pops?
3:	Ice Poles?
2:	Is Angel Delight an appropriate pudding?
1:	Is Carrot Cake an inappropriate pudding?

3:	Does Courgette belong in a cake?
JANE:	Yes, Yes and No.
1:	Does Brunch exist in your world?
JANE:	I call it elevenses *(laughs)*

General muttering confusion and repetition of the number '11' and the world 'elevenses' over emphasising different syllables and vowels so it slowly becomes a cacophony of confused noises.

Beat.

2:	Do you shit in public toilets?
JANE:	No.
1:	Very good.
3:	Do you wee in Urinals?
JANE:	Not as a woman.
3:	As a woman?
JANE:	Well, we use the stalls.
3:	Some women use them.
JANE:	What?
3:	The urinals. To wee in.

Beat.

1:	Do you think Mrs Brown's Boys is quality entertainment?
3:	Do you like Ant & Dec?
2:	Do you vote on X-factor?
JANE:	Yes, Yes and No.

2:	Do you watch it?
JANE:	No.
3:	Not even the first few episodes?
1:	They help your people.
2:	We all laugh at your people.
JANE:	That's the problem.
1:	Do you love Staffordshire Bull Terriers?
2:	Do you prefer Lino over carpet?
3:	Was McDonalds only a birthday treat?
1:	Did you call your neighbours Auntie & Uncle?
2:	Do you steal the free sugar from hotels?
3:	Or service stations?
1:	Or Starbucks?
JANE:	I don't go to Starbucks.
1:	Well done. That was a trick question.
2 & 3:	*They clap JANE*
1:	What do you do when it's cold?
JANE:	Put the heating on.
3:	Tut Tut Tut.
2:	You should put more clothes on.
1:	Do you say 'sack the juggler' whenever anyone drops anything?
3:	Do you use a nailbrush?

2:	Do you call Water – Council Pop?
1:	Did you ever get your haircut by your Mom's friend?
JANE:	I did actually yes.
2:	Very good.
3:	Was a bus stop your main social meeting point?
2:	Do you call every *baby* you see Baba, Bubba, Bubs or Bab-E?
1:	Do you tan before going abroad?
2:	Do you tan until your skin is leather?
3:	Do you clean your house before going on holiday?
1:	Do you think Oliver Twist had it lucky?
3:	Do you frown on Billy Elliot for attending a private dance school?
2:	Do you know that only the middle/upper classes can pluck you from obscurity?
1:	Do you live life with little to no hope?
3:	Are you content in not being bothered by the clear superiority those finically better off?
2:	Do you think progressive thinking is competitive?
3:	Are you ready to embrace the new cultures that will be introduced to you?

1:	And have you adjusted your life's narrative appropriately enough to wear the badge of the degradation and neglect about your awful upbringing?
JANE:	I did <u>not</u> have an awful upbringing.

Beat.

3:	What?
JANE:	I didn't have an awful upbringing. There was no degradation or neglect.
2:	There must.
3:	I don't understand.
JANE:	My upbringing was extremely positive. I lived in a house with people who loved me. I loved them. They raised me and made me who I am. They made me, and I am happy being me.
2:	You're happy?
JANE:	Yes.
3:	Being you?
JANE:	Definitely.
1:	Are you sure?
JANE:	Yes.
1:	That's positive.
2:	Very positive.
3:	Extremely positive.
JANE:	Good I'm really glad that's cleared up.

1:	We love your optimism.

The interviewers slowly begin putting the table and themselves in order – wiping off make-up, putting food away and returning to the naturalistic state and their RP accent returns

JANE:	Is there a problem?
2:	That goes against our criteria.
1:	We can't help you escape, be the brand and live in Cow-Cac if you are happy where you reside.
3:	If you are happy about where you came from.
2:	Are you happy?
JANE:	As a pig in shit.
3:	Sorry what?
JANE:	I'm really happy about who I am, who I have become and where I have come from.
1:	Well I think that brings this interview to an end.
3:	Sorry Jane but we have expectations you need to meet before we help you.
2:	Sorry Jane but we have standards we expect from you before we can pity you.
1:	These are just the basic requirements before we can patronise you.
3:	Do you understand?
JANE:	No, not particularly.
1:	Its all about Em …

2 & 3:	...POW ..
1:	... erment. You can leave now.

JANE stands.

3:	Sorry Jane.
2:	Jane Shade.
1:	Remember Jane, it's a marathon, not a sprint.
3:	It's a canal barge, not a rowing boat.
2:	It's a ladder, not an escalator.
1:	Don't stop climbing those rungs. You'll see us up there when you do.
2:	Looking down on you.
3:	Cheering you on. Patting you on head
2:	Come on Jane Shade, you can do it.
1:	We're done here. Good luck with your future endeavours Jane Shade.
2:	Ta'ra, Ta'ra, Ta'ra.

Blackout.

THE END

NSA

by Charles Entsie

(…) Indicates a pause/silence.

It's nearly midnight. MAN and BOY are sat in the car with tinted windows. It's parked in a Cineworld underground car park and has been for some time.

BOY: I've got one oldest sister. Two older brothers…
              Mum lives in Wood Green. Dad lives in Ghana.

              Divorced.

              You?

MAN: Two older Sisters. Cousins obviously/but they
              live back home so – Mum lives in Croydon.

BOY: /oh yeah same forgot.

              …

BOY: Calm

              …

BOY: Your headlights are on I think

(MAN checks.)

MAN: Nah not mine, must be the lights on the wall
              or summin init

BOY: Oh kl

              …

MAN: So does your sister know?

BOY: Nah

MAN: Suspect anything?

BOY: Don't think so you know. I don't think I
              make it obvious

              …

              Yours?

MAN:	Nah probably not. No reason to.
	What about the rest of your family?
BOY:	Brothers. Dunno. One went through my things found something. Made up some excuse though
MAN:	What
BOY:	That it's for some theatre show I'm doing at sixth form, a prop init –
MAN:	*(Laughs.)* You're bad
BOY:	Just good at keeping secrets init

(BOY's phone repeatedly vibrates but he ignores this.)

…

	Errm yh and don't think my Mum does or she just chooses to ignore it. She's in her fifties, says she just wants her happiness now with some guy she's just met so ignores most things
MAN:	Seen
BOY:	Your mum?
MAN:	Nah. No reason to.

…

BOY:	What would she do though? If she clocked?

…

MAN:	Don't even know. Don't know if I care that much anymore. Live alone, old enough to be doing what I want/
BOY:	/True

MAN:	Harder for you though init, cos u still live with yours
BOY:	Yh but making enough money now so I'll be out soon, rent my own place init
MAN:	From doing this?
BOY:	Yh
MAN:	Seen…How much you make a day?

Silence.

MAN:	Said you were going to uni last time I swear
BOY:	Yeah soon in September
MAN:	To study what
BOY:	Economics and Business hopefully
MAN:	Makes sense, doubt u need it
BOY:	What do you mean
MAN:	You already got a business going on here init
BOY:	This aint legit though
MAN:	Yeah?
BOY:	So I can't be always doing this
MAN:	So what would u wanna do
BOY:	Maybe work in the city or something. Get to wear nice suits and stuff. Commute every day. Bit of certainty.
MAN:	What's uncertain bout this

Pause.

BOY: These lot will be here one day, then the next
             their gettin "baptised","born again", "turning
             over a new leaf', therapy, support group,
             one of them tings...good for them and that
             init, but then obviously it's people like me
             who start to lose out...even if it is only just
             for a while and then they're usually back...
             still fucks with business...u know, customer
             loyalty...repeat purchases...all of that kinda
             shit/

MAN: /Hold on

Pause.

(MAN turns off the interior light.)

Silence.

MAN*:*   Gone I think

Pause.

MAN: So you'd rather make probably half of what
             u get now. Just to take a train every morning
             with complete strangers pressed up against
             you. And to stare at some computer screen
             most of the day

BOY: Parts of that aint nothing new to me tho….
             and will be legit

Pause.

MAN: Trust me it aint all that.

MAN lights up a zoot and starts smoking.

Silence.

             Let me tell u summin man. People like to go
             on about things being legit, doing this legit,

doing that legit, but whats the point of all of dat if you end up losing out even more. End up worse off…

Government takes a massive chunk of whatever u make to not do the shit they said they would do, or be greedy and use some cheap shit that in a few years ends up fucking us all or killing people. No point of following the rules when the people who made the rules or at the very least, are meant to… uphold them, don't follow them there-selves.

BOY appears to be taking this in but is unwavered.

MAN offers zoot to BOY - BOY declines.

MAN: You don't pay tax from the stuff your doing here init?/ Okay. So why would u wanna pay it making even less? Cos it's right? Cos it's fair?

BOY: /Noo

(BOY is unable to articulate his reasoning but his actions are as if to say "It's just what you're supposed to do init.")

MAN: You're a young black guy who lives in Wood Green, in tower blocks where ppl are getting knifed and gunned down left right and centre and nothing's being done bout that. They close down more youth clubs and shit. Make shit harder for us nd then get on to us for doing what we have to do. *That* aint fair. At your age you shouldn't have to be worryin bout the shit you've been telling me bout

BOY: I know man but, it is what it is is init

Pause.

MAN gazes at BOY. He then proceeds to take another smoke of the zoot.

MAN: Fuck being legit…

BOY: Dunno bout that man

MAN: Legit gets you by. Legit gets you what you
            need, not what you want. Legit doesn't
            mean even being comfortable nowadays.
            It's selfish. To yourself bruv, ur family – legit
            means a limit in providing for your family.
            Legit means helping your mum out with the
            bills every now and then rather than buying
            her that house, mansion she's dreamt of….

            Get there and she's still wearing the same
            hair net, using the same pot with the same
            spoon, on the same stove, to cook ur
            favourite food in. Not even asking the same
            questions bout your life anymore, that you
            used the same techniques to avoid before.
            She's talking bout someone elses kid doing
            bits, you clock their age and try change the
            subject…and when she's done, goes back to
            bed in the same room, with the same curtains
            covered in layers of raid, wearing pyjamas
            with the same bleach stain on the sleeve, in
            the bed with the same mattress, light fading
            away from that same window, with birdshit
            on a different spot each morning, gets ready
            to go to the same place…

Pause.

            And ur back in the same room, from when u
            were a Boy… tryna find something to take ur
            mind off shit…same time tryna track which
            fucking decision on what day at what time
            led u here, to this moment…just tryna…

NSA   28   CHARLES ENTSIE

…survive. Survive? …

…Humans aint been prey since what like… Sixty-five million years ago when the fuckin dinosaurs died out. Swr were the fuckin predators now? We don't just survive man. Were supposed to live man, fucking thrive.

Silence

BOY: You know most people just come for what
                they paid for and go

(Laughs.)

BOY: But yh man…kinda get what you're saying
                but still – You never know init…anything
                could happen.

MAN: Yeah exactly and that's what I'm saying,
                you can't be going for certain job cos it's
                "certain", nothing is "certain" so you need to
                do what the fuck you *want* to do now init

Pause.

                (Sombrely.) Regret about the consequences later

Pause.

                Trust me, I know what I'm chatting about g.

BOY: Yolo init

MAN: Yo even I know that "yolo" phrase is dead

Laughs.

BOY: How are your windows still steamy/– *(Phone
                suddenly vibrates repeatedly again. BOY finally
                checks it.)*

MAN:	/We can't really be rolling the windows down tho init/
BOY:	/Shit…Got to go now man
MAN:	…*(Disappointedly.)* Yhyh course

(MAN goes in his pockets.)

MAN:	I gave u the money at the start init, 100
BOY:	Yhyh for an hour, you did
MAN:	Cool…here take another fifty, feels like I took bit more than an hour talking and shit
BOY:	U sure
MAN:	Yhyh man
BOY:	Thanks man

(BOY does up his belt and proceeds to get out the car then hesitates.)

BOY:	And 'llow it man next time take that off init lol *(Gestures ring finger.)* …feels bare weird *doing it* and seeing that on your finger
MAN:	Oh shit
BOY:	Nah don't worry it's cool man, remember I'm good at keeping secrets
	Safe
MAN:	…

(Door shuts. Car engine starts. But the car remains stationary. MAN is sat still for a moment before readjusting his clothes properly and spraying himself with his cologne. He then proceeds to leave. Lights go dark…)

LA MERDE

by Roberta Livingston

Characters

CHRISSY
Female, Black, 21

DEX
Male, Gay, Any race/ethnicity, 20

MACKENZIE
Female, Mixed-Race, 21

ALLEGRA ALDRIDGE
Female, White, 33

NOTES

Speech interruptions are marked with a −

When Chrissy talks to the audience directly, the
action on stage freezes.

PROLOGUE

MACKENZIE walks to centre stage. She takes a couple of breaths and a spotlight shines on her. As the scene progresses we see her desperation come to surface.

MACKENZIE: *(Breathy.)*

> Hi I'm Mackenzie Thompson, I'm twenty-one, from Essex

Ding.

> I am the perfect person for this role because I have a current look

Ding.

> I'm not your stereotypical model

Ding.

> I'm motivated and hungry

Ding.

> I'm knowledgeable

Ding.

> I know this industry inside out

Ding.

> Ever since I was a little girl I would play with my Mum's make-up

Ding.

> I promise I will not let you down

Ding.

> I am this brand

Ding.

This brand is me

Ding.

You want me to pose?

Ding.

She strikes a pose

Ding.

She strikes a pose

Ding.

She strikes a pose

Ding.

I promise I –

Ding.

Thank you for your time.

Beat.

MACKENZIE looks up.

MACKENZIE: Mum?

Blackout.

SCENE ONE

CHRISSY and DEX both run onto stage from opposite ends. CHRISSY pulls out her phone, calls DEX.

DEX: *(Answering the phone.)* Chrissy I haven't watched it yet!

CHRISSY: Neither have I!

DEX: So why you belling up my phone please?

CHRISSY: I just –

DEX: Shh!

CHRISSY: But when –

DEX: Shhh!

CHRISSY: Dex!

DEX: Girl, bye. Call me after!

DEX hangs up.

CHRISSY: *(To audience.)* You guys have no idea how big
                  of a deal today is!

*They turn on their laptops. The 'Apple sound' fills the space. They
both fiercely type which is interrupted by the dramatic entrance of
ALLEGRA ALDRIDGE. Runway music plays, sounds similar to the
America's Next Top Model soundtrack. CHRISSY & DEX sing along.*

CHRISSY & DEX: *(Sings.)* For you but better, for the better
                  you!

ALLEGRA: Hi I'm Allegra Aldridge founder, CEO and
                  Creative Director of *La Merde Beauty.*

DEX: That's right tell 'em girl!

CHRISSY: She's the ultimate girl boss! *(to audience)*
                  Allegra Aldridge is the biggest YouTube
                  Beauty sensation the platform has ever seen
                  with a massive cult following of twenty
                  million subscribers. I have modelled my
                  business plan after hers; I want to do what
                  she does. I want to create beautiful buttery
                  lipsticks, sensational shadows that are
                  swatch-worthy for the gods, magnificent

	mascaras that will volumise lashes up to Jesus! You catching my drift? She's *the* shit!
ALLEGRA:	I know many of you have been waiting a while for this announcement and I am thrilled that the countdown has come to an end.
CHRISSY:	Please be a new foundation!
DEX:	Better be a new foundation!
ALLEGRA:	I am proud to present *La Merde Beauty's* brand new collection of ColourMask Foundations.

CHRISSY & DEX both scream in excitement.

	This dewy matte finish foundation is designed to last for twenty-four hours. That's right you heard me correctly – Twenty. Four. Hours.
DEX:	Oh my gahh
ALLEGRA:	The full collection of the ColourMask Foundations will be available December 14th in all good cosmetic stores.
CHRISSY:	That's like three weeks away!
ALLEGRA:	But for all you eager beauty fans out there, I will be hosting an exclusive event at Selfridges this Wednesday 28th November 12 noon. Not only to celebrate the new ColourMask Foundations but to reveal our new *La Merde* girl for this special campaign.

CHRISSY and DEX gasp.

The first twenty people to queue at the Selfridges Main Entrance on Wednesday will get a wristband, which not only gains you entry to the private event but also a complimentary bottle of the brand new ColourMask Foundation. I hope to see your beautiful faces there. Lots of love, Allegra Aldridge *(blows kisses)*

CHRISSY & DEX catch them. ALLEGRA exits. CHRISSY calls DEX.

CHRISSY: Dex –

DEX screams.

CHRISSY: Dex –

DEX screams.

CHRISSY: Dex, calm down!

DEX: Babe we have to go to the event!

CHRISSY: Duhh! I have a million questions to ask Allegra! And omg imagine all of the industry people that will be there that I can show my business plan to!

DEX: That's right girl you get them contacts! What are you gonna wear? I need to know so I can co-ordinate.

CHRISSY: I'm thinking my jumpsuit, that screams Beauty. Business. Woman. Don't you think?

DEX: What, the one you wore to Zak's party and Mackenzie Thompson was wearing the exact same jumpsuit so she pushed you into a pool of Aleesha Nixon's vomit?

CHRISSY: Erm, no! I got a new one from ASOS actually. Thanks for bringing up that painful memory though, such a great friend.

DEX:	Sorry, my bad. It was jokes though even though I hate Mackenzie Thompson.
CHRISSY:	Everyone hates Mackenzie Thompson.
DEX:	Well not really. Everyone on social media loves her, you two just had that archnemesis thing goin' on.
CHRISSY:	*(Outburts to audience.)* She thinks she's the it-girl now because she got scouted in Primark, dropped out of uni and signed a model contract. Perlease, I couldn't care less that you're in the new Missguided advert. Pft. Like whatever. Zero f's given. Pfffft. Her eyes are two different sizes anyway so…
DEX:	Chrissy! You still there?
CHRISSY:	Yep! Anyways – back to the jumpsuit, it's like an electric blue colour and tailored.
DEX:	Sick! I will make sure my outfit will compliment yours.
CHRISSY:	Thank you boo.
DEX:	You know I got you girl.
CHRISSY:	Okay next thing. Wristbands. First twenty people. That's not a lot. I feel like some extra as hell people will be camping out from the early hours. I'm not on that.
DEX:	I ain't either. I need my beauty sleep.
CHRISSY:	Hmm. My Uncle Kwame is a security guard at Selfridges he usually does the opening time shift during the week. I'll ask him, I'm sure he can get us two.

DEX: Eyyyy, Uncle Kwame! Okay, perfect. *(Screams.)* I'm so excited! I need to buy some fresh beauty blenders so that beautiful foundation can grace my fabulous face.

CHRISSY: Ugh, I feel you! Are you coming in tomorrow?

DEX: Do I ever go to Professor Millstone's lectures? I am not sitting in front of that homophobic obese white man for two hours watching him teach me from a textbook that I can read at home.

CHRISSY: You never study at home though?

DEX: That ain't the point Chrissy! The point is I'm not going in! Sign me in though please?

CHRISSY: Of course Dex. Okay so I'll see you on Wednesday? Meet me at the main entrance at 11.30?

DEX: 'kay babe, see you there! Ciao! Mwah.

CHRISSY: Bye babe. Mwah.

CHRISSY ends the call to DEX and then calls her Uncle Kwame. As she speaks on the phone to him she exits.

CHRISSY: Hi Uncle it's Chrissy. Chrissy! Your niece? C-H-R-I- Yes! Your niece. Listen Uncle, I need a huge favour please.

Blackout.

SCENE TWO

La Merde Beauty's event. There is a high table with little gift bags on them and on the opposite side is a poster covered with a sheet. Runway music plays. ALLEGRA ALDRIDGE is holding a glass of champagne and talking to MACKENZIE THOMPSON. CHRISSY & DEX enter looking chic, both wearing neon yellow wristbands. Holding hands they take in the fabulous event.

DEX: O.M.G babe! This place looks amazing!

CHRISSY: I know right! I can't believe we actually
              made it in, I owe Uncle Kwame big time.
              Oh, look! Allegra Aldridge is over there.

DEX: She looks so hot, that third facelift did her
              well.

CHRISSY: Uh huh. Wait who's she talking to – that's not
              who I think it is, is it?

DEX: *(Belts out.)* Oh my god it's Mackenzie!

CHRISSY: *(Whispers.)* Shhhhhhhhh Dex, what the hell?

MACKENZIE looks over. They try to hide their faces.

DEX: She must be the new *La Merde* girl!

CHRISSY: No pffft it can't be her.

ALLEGRA unveils the poster with MACKENZIE's face on it.

CHRISSY: Okay so it is her.

DEX: It's okay babe.

CHRISSY: I mean her face is not even symmetrical –

DEX: Forget about her – look *(he sees the table of little
              gift bags)* these must be the complimentary
              foundations.

DEX guides CHRISSY over to the table. They begin to look through the bags.

CHRISSY:　　　　Hmmm, this is weird I can't seem to find my shade.

DEX:　　　　It's all Fifty Shades of Beige up in here.

MACKENZIE spots them and slithers over.

MACKENZIE:　　Well well look what the binmen left behind…

CHRISSY:　　　*(To audience.)* Tad cliché

(Back to MACKENZIE.)

　　　　　　Mackenzie.

MACKENZIE:　　Christine.

CHRISSY:　　　It's Chriss –

MACKENZIE:　　Awww look how cute you guys are with your little wristbands, scavenging off the freebies.

DEX:　　　　Just leave us alone Mackenzie we are not here to bother you.

MACKENZIE:　　Well you are *bothering* me!

DEX:　　　　BIIIIIITTTTTCHHHH? Is that my problem? You came over here with your gangly legs and dragon breath all up in our personal space –

CHRISSY:　　　Dex! She's not worth it, come on let's go, let's go ask Allegra where our shades at.

MACKENZIE:　　*(Sniggers.)* Good luck with that.

CHRISSY:　　　What's that supposed to mean?

MACKENZIE:　　Wake up Christine!

CHRISSY:	It's Chriss –
MACKENZIE:	You. Poster. *You*. Poster. Now think about the foundation shades in those bags. *La Merde Beauty* encapsulates elegance, luxury and sophistication.
CHRISSY:	What are you saying?
MACKENZIE:	I'm saying *this* is Selfridges. Maybe you should try Savers for your shade.
CHRISSY:	You're saying I'm too dark?
MACKENZIE:	*(Patronisingly pats her)* I'm sorry hun –
CHRISSY:	Don't touch me!
DEX:	Do not touch her!
CHRISSY:	*(To the audience.)* Shit. What do I do now? I'm here. I'm finally here in this room with Allegra Aldridge and so many industry people that could help me with my business. Take me to the next level.

Okay.

Breathe.

If we bump into her, don't say anything. Just don't say anything. Just say hello, smile, congratulate her on the foundations and walk away. Walk away, don't cause a scene. Don't show yourself up in front of all these important people.

This is not fair. This is so not fair. No. I'm gonna say something, yeah I'm gonna say something. I'm gonna just state the facts. I'll say Allegra you racist piece of shi–.

> *(Suppresses her anger.)* I'll say, *politely*, Allegra, where are the foundations for people like me? I'll wait for her reply. Which will be some BS excuse like "the deeper shades are still in the production phase" but I won't get angry I'll keep my cool. I'll keep my cool and I'll explain to her how horrific she has made me feel.
>
> F that! Why should I have to educate her on racial equality? I'm not a bloody teacher. I'm not getting paid to teach a white woman on how to be inclusive. Like is it really that hard? Is it really that hard to make a foundation collection with a wide shade range? No it's not! She's just wrapped up in her privilege!
>
> Okay calm down, calm yourself down Chrissy.

Beat. (She thinks.)

> I am not going to say anything.

MACKENZIE: What's the matter Christine? Still want to ask Allegra where your shades are?

CHRISSY: No it's fine we are going to leave any–

MACKENZIE: Allegra!

CHRISSY: Shut up Mackenzie!

MACKENZIE: Allegra darling, over here sweetie.

ALLEGRA glides over.

ALLEGRA: Yes, Mackenzie darling?

CHRISSY is frozen.

MACKENZIE:	Please meet my friends Christine and Dex.
DEX:	*(Aside.)* Erm who said we were frie–
ALLEGRA:	*(Distastefully)* Pleasure.
MACKENZIE:	Little Christine has a question for you, don't you Christine?
CHRISSY:	*(To the audience.)* Fuck it.

(To ALLEGRA with 100% conviction) Where is my foundation?

DEX is awakened at this new confident CHRISSY and gets his phone out and begins to film.

ALLEGRA:	Excuse me?
CHRISSY:	My foundation? Your range seems to lack the shades of the beautiful black persuasion.
ALLEGRA:	*(Stumbles.)* Well the uh, the uh, the blacker shades, I mean *deeper* shades are still in the production phase –

CHRISSY looks at the audience in a "told you so" way.

CHRISSY:	Disappointment doesn't even begin to describe all the things I want to say to you. You were my idol Allegra. An independent woman who built her brand from nothing. You're just another one of *them.*
ALLEGRA:	I'm not a racis–
CHRISSY:	*(Laughs)* Yeah, okay. Allegra Aldridge. Because you have a mixed-race face for your new campaign means you couldn't possibly be racist.
ALLEGRA:	I'm sorry but I don't know who the hell you are –

CHRISSY:	I'm your biggest competitor. Maybe not right now but this time in a year I will be. And my business will run yours into the ground.
DEX:	The ground!
ALLEGRA:	*(Laughs.)* A year? Oh now that really is sweet, thinking you could do this in one year.
CHRISSY:	Watch me.

CHRISSY goes to exit, MACKENZIE blocks her.

MACKENZIE:	*(Outraged)* Christine I can't believe you just called Allegra the "r-word"!
CHRISSY:	My name is Chrissy.

CHRISSY punches the poster right through MACKENZIE's face. MACKENZIE bursts into tears.

ALLEGRA:	*(Screams.)* SECURITY! SECURITY!
CHRISSY:	Uncle Kwame it's good! I'm good! I'm good. Dex, let's go!
ALLEGRA:	*(Screams)* SECURITY! DO SOMETHING, I WANT HER ARRESTED! SECURITY! HELLO?

CHRISSY exits and DEX follows her still filming. MACKENZIE is still crying.

DEX:	We got you bitches!

DEX exits.

THE END

PAPA

by Sid Sagar

Characters

RAVI

50s, male, South Asian.

LAYLA

20s, female, mixed race (White/South Asian).

SCENE 1

Lights up.

RAVI, alone on stage. He speaks directly to us.

RAVI: I was seven, I think, when I went to my first cricket match. The Feroz Shah Kotla Ground in Delhi. There is something about the smell that stays with me today. The dust from the turf. The dryness. Maybe cow dung too – I think they used it on the grass. Oil. Cooking oil. Impossible to escape. Onions. A lot of onions. So many men pressed together. The pits. You know? Armpit stench. It is powerful. Consuming. I forget the match but remember the smell.

Beat.

We walk home. It is still light. The air, hazy. Smoke and sun and maybe shit, too. The magic Delhi air. When they talk today about the smog and the air and the global warming they forget about the beauty, I think. The way light can force through the cloud and the dirt and suddenly in a back street behind a market you see things you have never seen before. In one of these streets, beyond Paharganj, maybe near Old Delhi, I think, behind the Jama Masjid, Papa says "Their holy place here, bache, and their beggars behind, look, dekh! Holy place and beggars, side by side!" But this was all of Delhi, I thought. It is. At the traffic light children in Manchester United shirts, the red now brown, hair in knots, knocking on the windows of the Ambassador cars and

the fancy people will not look. But I loved
Papa's stories and how he told them. Always
a shine in his eye. So I listened. And I
believed. Maybe people will always believe
until a moment when truth happens and
they cannot believe the same thing.

Beat.

Papa hit a beggar girl on the way home
from cricket. Her scarf on her head fell,
I remember. The knock of his hand on
her cheek was like a bat on a ball, in the
sweet spot. It was a full knock. Hollow and
cracked. Her blood was bright, and dark,
and flowing as thickly as the Yamuna in
the monsoon. Her scarf on the ground, it
was dusty now, there was dirt on the beads
which maybe her grandmother had stitched
on as a decoration, and the drip of blood on
the muddy floor had made the brown into
a red, a dirty red, like the children at the
traffic light in the Manchester United shirts.

Lights down.

SCENE 2

Lights up.

A modest living room: a small sofa, some chairs, a coffee table with coasters and a couple of magazines.

RAVI sits on the sofa. He rearranges the coasters and magazines, attempting to neaten them.

The sound of a flush.

LAYLA enters.

RAVI:	All okay?
LAYLA:	What?
RAVI:	All okay?
LAYLA:	What do you mean?
RAVI:	Just making a check up.
LAYLA:	I'm fine, yeah.
RAVI:	It's a new flush.

Beat.

	The toilet.
LAYLA:	That's great.
RAVI:	I'm unsure about the quality of the handyman's work. He was recommended. From work.
LAYLA:	Good to know.

Beat.

RAVI:	Have you seen Rogue Traders?

LAYLA:	Rogue Traders?
RAVI:	You've watched it?
LAYLA:	Nope.
RAVI:	It's excellent. It gave me the idea of perhaps observing the craftsmanship of Gary.
LAYLA:	You mean, spying on the guy who fitted the flush?
RAVI:	Yes, exactly.
LAYLA:	So I'd guess you have to install cameras?
RAVI:	Precisely.
LAYLA:	In the loo?
RAVI:	I suppose, yes. To ensure transparency. Efficient service. Prevent a scam, you know?
LAYLA:	Bit fucking weird, if I'm honest. Cameras in the loo.

Beat.

RAVI:	Layla, may I hug you?
LAYLA:	Sorry?
RAVI:	May I. Hug you?
LAYLA:	Jesus.
RAVI:	What?
LAYLA:	Don't be creepy.
RAVI:	I wasn't –
LAYLA:	Mum is two minutes away. In the car. All I have to do is call her and as soon as she sees

	my name pop up she'll know something's wrong and she'll be here and she'll fucking smash you up.
RAVI:	I understand, I just…I want to give you a hug.
LAYLA:	You sound mental. Like fucking…Siri.
RAVI:	Okay. I'm sorry.

LAYLA sits on a chair and glances at the magazines.

RAVI:	Helen's choices.
LAYLA:	She seems cultured.
RAVI:	She is. She reads a lot. Books, I mean. I try too but it is harder, you know?
LAYLA:	I don't, actually.
RAVI:	You have always been an intelligent one.
LAYLA:	You don't know that.
RAVI:	I do.
LAYLA:	You've got no clue.
RAVI:	I read online. About you. And also what you write.
LAYLA:	Don't lie.
RAVI:	I'm not. I think it's highly impressive. I cannot write the way you write.
LAYLA:	Have you stalked me?
RAVI:	What?
LAYLA:	You stalked me online, yeah?

RAVI:	I am interested, yes.
LAYLA:	That's how you found my email?
Beat.	
LAYLA:	What have you read?
RAVI:	The…the articles. On the. It's a big website.
LAYLA:	Great. I believe you now.
RAVI:	Inter. Section.
LAYLA:	What?
RAVI:	Intersection.
LAYLA:	Intersectionality?
RAVI:	Precisely.
LAYLA:	What about it?
RAVI:	I like that one. Very much.
Beat.	
	'The Bravery of the Burka. How Islamic Feminists are Paving the Way for a Brighter Future.'
Beat.	
	This one was beautiful. I think. I did a comment.
LAYLA:	What?
RAVI:	Online. The website. I did a comment on the article.
LAYLA:	What did you say?

RAVI:	There was a comment from Barry_ ItsComingHome12. It was mean, I think. Ill-guided.
LAYLA:	Ill-informed.
RAVI:	Ill-informed. About Islam. And this country. And what it means to be part of the country. I said it is very simple thing to attack the habit of one without a voice. So when the voice is given a space to speak it is not a challenge, or an opponent, but maybe a space to talk and understand.

Beat.

Six likes.

LAYLA smiles.

LAYLA:	That's not bad.
RAVI:	Barry did a comment.
LAYLA:	What did he say?
RAVI:	"Fuck you Gavaskar you wet blanket suck on Owen Jones".
LAYLA:	What's Gavaskar?
RAVI:	My profile name. A cricketer. Amazing cricketer.

He goes to a cabinet and opens a drawer. He takes out an envelope.

RAVI:	For you.
LAYLA:	What is it?
RAVI:	Open it.

LAYLA:	If it's a letter you can just tell me what it says.
RAVI:	Not a letter.

She opens the envelope and takes out a credit card.

RAVI:	The PIN has not arrived but when it does I will forward it.

Beat.

There is no limit. You can use it and there is no limit to the amount.

Beat.

There is a link, I think, to the Nectar points. So if you spend you will have points too.

LAYLA:	Fuck.
RAVI:	Sorry?
LAYLA:	Fuck this.
RAVI:	What do you mean, sweetheart?
LAYLA:	Don't you dare call me sweetheart. You... you fucking...don't ever call me sweetheart. Don't ever do that. Do you understand? Do you fucking understand me?

Beat.

I can't. I can't do this. Oh God.

RAVI:	Layla, please, bache, sit.
LAYLA:	Don't call me bache!
RAVI:	Okay. I'm sorry, Layla. I'm sorry.

Beat.

LAYLA:	You can't even afford this.
RAVI:	I –
LAYLA:	You can't. Even if you wanted to.
RAVI:	I will afford this. It is the only thing I will afford. I want you to take it. I need you to take it and if you want to put it away in the locker or in wherever and cut it into pieces you can do all these things but I need you to take it. Please, Layla. My Layla. I need this to happen. It is all I need.

Beat.

LAYLA:	Mum and I lived, for a few years, in this village in Bedfordshire. A proper shithole. And I remember this group, maybe a gang, I suppose, of Asian boys who lived in the next village. And they noticed me, I think. They did. They could see something in me. On my face, maybe. A shine. That I was, sort of, part of them, and yet I wasn't, really. And those Asian boys knew they could get to me and one day, it was the end of term I think, I was with my friend Becca who was coming back to mine after school and this lanky boy with the hint of a moustache and dandruff on his blazer said something to me and the other boys laughed and I remember looking at Becca first, lovely Becca who was always so kind and was the first person to speak to me when I started at that school and showed me where the registers were kept, and she looked terrified. I can't remember what he said, I don't think I heard what he said, not properly, but I

remember turning around and walking up to him. And in his eyes I saw fear, I think. There was something detached and vacant and so sad about his eyes. His skin was dry, and scaly too. I could see it, from around his neck. I was young but it was incredible, actually, how powerful I felt. I saw something in that boy and I knew, then, that he was sad and rejected and probably as angry as the white boys who played football at the Rec and got into fights and it was obvious, actually, that those boys were the same. In that village in Bedfordshire. They were lost, I reckon. I hope they've found meaning, those boys.

Beat.

I needed you. I need you. To hug me. Please.

Lights down.

END.

GODFREY

by Aisling Towl

Characters

SIMONE

21, from South London. Friendly. Her focus is always on the
room.

JASON

23, from South London. Serious. His focus is always on the
donuts.

CARYS

29, from Devon. Unsure. Her focus is always outside the room.

GODFREY

40, from Buckinghamshire. Unabashed. His focus is always
himself.

SETTING

2018. Godfrey's, a French 'Fast Food' Restaurant in Streatham,
South London. Young, expensive, hipster casual, think independent Leon. They definitely do boozy brunch on weekends, meals
probably ranging from £7 – £14. The food is good. There are
playlists. They are concerned with manufacturing an atmosphere.

All scenes take place within one working day, a Tuesday, but there
are never any customers. Scenes take place before, after and on
breaks within the shift. When characters are not present in the
scenes they are elsewhere in the restaurant, apart from Godfrey
who is not in the restaurant until his arrival in scene three.

The time of each scene is stated at the beginning and should be
made known to the audience.

A "–" in the text indicates where a character is interrupted

A "/" in the text indicates where two characters' speech overlaps

PROLOGUE

8:55am.

Enter JASON to an empty staff room, turns on lights which flicker and then settle. Puts his things away, gets ready for work with some level of routine, puts kettle on.

Notices a box of donuts on the table. They are not his. He looks to see if any are left, thinks about taking one. Decides not to. Continues getting ready. Goes back to the donuts, reconsidering. Is about to take one, when –

Enter CARYS. JASON jumps back from the donuts, which causes CARYS also to jump.

CARYS:	Hello/ I'm Carys.
JASON:	Are these yours?

Pause.

JASON:	People shouldn't leave things here overnight because we sometimes get rodents.
CARYS:	Oh.

Pause.

JASON:	Are you new?
CARYS:	Yes. Sorry. I'm a bit early. Is Godfrey here?
JASON:	No.
CARYS:	Okay.
JASON:	Godfrey doesn't work on Tuesdays.
CARYS:	Okay.
JASON:	Do you have a T-Shirt?

CARYS:	No.
JASON:	He didn't give you a T-shirt?
CARYS:	No.
JASON:	I think there's some in the cupboard.

CARYS puts her bag away. JASON looks at the donuts.

* * *

SCENE ONE

11.03am. The restaurant, pre shift brief/ pep-talk. JASON is explaining to CARYS. SIMONE is doing her make-up.

JASON:	We've got like, half an hour til we open so you lot can chill, grab a coffee, whatever. Basically, just remember that people don't just want a burger. They want an *experience*. I read an article yesterday about Foodies, you know, millennials, like me, us, like what they want, and it said when the meal is aesthetically pleasing, and like, photogenic, there's a release of dopamine from the brain which actually like, your taste cells, like, loosen their chemical bonds and break down the food enzymes better so it stimulates your, like, it tastes better.
CARYS:	Wow.
JASON:	Which is why we're all about presentation here. And taste.
SIMONE:	*(Laughing.)* What shit are you chatting, Jase? It's fine, Carys, babes, it's literally such a chill environment. If you fuck up just tell

	me and I'll cover for you, but to be honest, Godfrey's never in anyway.
JASON:	He's coming in today actually.
SIMONE:	What!? On a Tuesday?
JASON:	He just texted me. It's just to see me. He's thinking of going part time – like, more part time than he already is – and I'm due a promotion.
SIMONE:	I thought you were leaving?
JASON:	I am leaving. At the end of the financial year.
SIMONE:	He actually said he wanted a meeting with me last time I saw him. But he never –
JASON:	Oh great. So classic. You'll get it because you're a chick.
SIMONE:	Jase! I won't! I don't want it!

CARYS has been standing awkwardly between them. She now moves awkwardly to a chair and gets out her book.

JASON:	He'll give it to you though. Why don't you want it? Extra three pound an hour.
CARYS:	I thought Godfrey was gay.
JASON:	Godfrey's not *gay*. He's just eccentric. Wow.
SIMONE:	I don't have time because of uni.
JASON:	I don't have time because of my fashion line, Simone, but you have to hustle in this life, or this life hustles you. I should have been on supervisor rates since months ago, I always do till and closing.

SIMONE: I do till and closing too.

CARYS looks up for a moment, as if she is trying to remember something. Back to her book.

JASON: He's such a weird guy, man. I mentioned
                 I was thinking of cutting down my meat
                 intake for this gym plan like, once, and now
                 he sends me all these vegan conspiracy
                 videos on Whatsapp. He just invited me to
                 an animal rights march?

SIMONE: You should go!

JASON: I don't see the point in marching. I don't
                 really do politics.

CARYS looks up from her book and stares into space.

SIMONE: Carys, what are you reading?

CARYS: Oh, it's just this thing my sister, it's not –

JASON tilts the book whilst its still in her hands and reads out the title.

JASON: 'Transformative Justice…Reconciliation…in
                 Personal Healing'

CARYS: Um. Sorry. Can I –

JASON: What is this, Carys?

CARYS: I don't –

SIMONE: Ohhh! Transformative model of Justice! I
                 did this at A-Level. Sociology.

                 Basically, Jase, it's like, looking at justice in
                 a critical way, and finding new ways to like,
                 actually deal with injustice? And looking at
                 offenders with a… compassionate lens. So,

	long term social change, oh…and abolishing prisons. I think. Yeah.
JASON:	Abolishing prisons? Mad. So you wanna have murderers and rapists where? Wandering the streets?
CARYS:	Sorry, um, sorry, can you –
JASON:	*(He now has complete hold of CARYS' book, flicking through it.)* Mad…That sounds kinda interesting…Yeah. That compassionate lens shit is bullshit though…if someone betrays you, cut them out. Small circles. Snip snip motherfucker.
SIMONE:	It's more about, um, shifting focus? Accountability? Carys?
CARYS:	Um. I guess it's just…shifting focus from punishment and incarceration for offenders…to like, looking at causes of crime within communities…but the book isn't really about, um, the law…it's kind of taking the idea of transformation and using those ideas to talk about pain and forgiveness, like, for personal problems. Personal healing. Rather than community. Although it's kind of saying they're like, the same thing.

A long pause.

SIMONE:	Can I borrow that book after you, Carys?
CARYS:	Um. Yeah.

A pause. JASON gives CARYS back the book.

JASON:	How's your boy, Simone?

SIMONE: Ohhh I'm done, Jase, he's trash, we're not
             speaking –

JASON: Again?

SIMONE: Listen. We were supposed to have date night
             tonight, he hasn't taken me out for ages. He
             said cinema, I was like that's boring, he was like
             what do you wanna do then. Anyway, basically
             I realised its Blood Moon tonight so –

JASON: It's blood what?

SIMONE: It's Blood Moon, it's like a lunar eclipse, but
             with Mars, it has really strong masculine
             energy and healing energy and it signifies,
             new beginnings, so I thought that's so
             perfect, we can go up Telegraph Hill and
             watch the blood moon together, because
             we've been on a break basically but we're
             not anymore so new beginnings, but he
             didn't want to.

JASON: He didn't want to climb up a muddy hill
             and look at a moon with you?

CARYS looks up. Stares into space.

SIMONE: Jase. The world is most peaceful when
             masculine and feminine energy are
             balanced, the Blood Moon is *Mars* coming
             into alignment with the *earth* moon –

JASON: That's bullshit.

SIMONE: It's not, trust me, it's Astrology.

CARYS goes back to her book.

JASON: How long have you two been fucking now?

SIMONE:	We've been seeing each other on and off since February.
JASON:	Six months. That's like, longer than my longest relationship.

(SIMONE looks satisfied.)

SIMONE:	Do you have a boyfriend, Carys?
CARYS:	No.
JASON:	Do you have a girlfriend?
CARYS:	No. I did have a boyfriend until recently, but we broke up.
JASON:	Why?
CARYS:	It's a long. We weren't compatible. I guess.
SIMONE:	Why?
CARYS:	I –
SIMONE:	Are you a Libra by any chance?
JASON:	*(Rolls his eyes, making a thing of it.)*
CARYS:	Yeah? I don't really. Yeah, how did you –
SIMONE:	I can just tell.
JASON:	What the fuck?
SIMONE:	Was he a Taurus by any chance?
CARYS:	I don't know.

SCENE TWO

4pm. SIMONE and CARYS are polishing cutlery, there is lots.

SIMONE: I'm not saying I fully believe it, but you know when you're watching YouTube at three in the morning and you get stuck in a bit of a hole...I just think you have to stay open minded. I don't actually think it's flat, I just, it's not a globe, you know?

You know when you see a plane cross the sky, and then like twenty minutes later the exact same plane crosses the sky again? That's not a coincidence. That's what I'm talking about.

Once you start noticing things like that you can't stop. It's worse when I'm high, I see everything.

Pause. SIMONE obviously wants CARYS to say something. CARYS focuses very hard on getting a bit of dirt off a spoon.

SIMONE: What's the worst thing you've ever done for money?

CARYS: Um. I don't know.

SIMONE: Okay, what's like, the worst thing you've ever done?

CARYS: I –

SIMONE: I was looking after my neighbour's cat once while she was on holiday. I just had to go in and feed the cat once every other day because she had one of those feeder tube things. You know the ones?

CARYS: The ones where you set a timer?

SIMONE: Yeah. So she went away for two weeks to
                Tenerife, and like a week and a half in she
                Whatsapped me asking how the cat was.
                Basically, I completely forgot I was meant to
                be feeding it, her front door keys had been
                in the bottom of my handbag for like, a
                week and a half. I fucking screamed Carys,
                I was on the bus by myself and I actually
                fucking screamed. I literally jumped off the
                bus and took an Uber to her house, even
                though in my head I was like this cat is
                dead, he's fucking dead, four paws in the air,
                he's got no chance.

                I get there, takes me about ten minutes to
                get in the door because she has like five
                million locks but I get in and the cat is there,
                thank fuck, I poured it the biggest bowl of
                cat food and water and just sat down and
                watched it eat. I was crying. The cat was
                crying too.

CARYS: Christ.

SIMONE: I don't feel guilty about it anymore though.
                Cats were wild animals originally. They can
                fend for themselves really. It's kind of mad
                that we even have pets. I think they must
                have like, Stockholm Syndrome.

CARYS: I guess.

                (Pause.)

                So…was that your worst thing you've done
                for money or just your worst thing?

SIMONE:	Oh, I guess both? I did used to work at Babestation though, on the phones. The shifts were ten pm to six am, you had a little booth in a big room, like a call centre. Twenty pounds an hour, double pay on Christmas eve.
CARYS:	Wow.
SIMONE:	Some girls dressed up sexy, to like, get more in the mood? But most of us were in trackies. I used to bring a hot water bottle when I was on my reds. And there was free tea and coffee and biscuits, sometimes they even had those chocolate Viennese ones.
CARYS:	The ones with chocolate in the middle?
SIMONE:	Yep.
CARYS:	That doesn't sound too bad.
SIMONE:	Yeah, but the customers on the phones were horrible. Some of the things they'd say to you, like I'm no angel, Carys, but I'm actually quite an old fashioned girl when it comes to the bedroom. I like to feel respected, even if it's rough? I like it rough but on some level I still want to feel respected.
CARYS:	That's fair enough.
SIMONE:	Anyway, I tolerated it for a while, these men saying how they wanted to hurt me, and stuff, but then I had this one call right at the end of a shift from this fucking psychopath talking in my ear about chainsaws, and I lost it. I shouted down the phone at him about

how he needed to learn some respect, and
he must of thought I was playing along or
something, he got worse, and then I lost
it even more and next thing I know the
manager's stood behind me because I've
been shouting and it's been heard in the
background of other people's calls and next
thing I know I'm crying and telling her I
don't want to work there and then next
thing I know I'm at home on my laptop
applying to work at Godfrey's and next
thing I know I'm here.

*CARYS seems as if she might be about to say something in response
and as she does, manages to knock all the clean cutlery onto the dirty
floor. She sighs and they both start picking it all up to clean again.*

CARYS: I think the worst thing I've ever done for
            money was my last job too. I worked for
            Oxfam.

SIMONE: Oxfam? Isn't that a nice job?

CARYS: Yeah, it was. Tea and coffee and biscuits
            and all that. I started there in December
            last year, which was two months before the
            whole Haiti thing...surfaced.

SIMONE: Is that the child prostitute thing?

CARYS: They, yeah, they weren't child prostitutes,
            not that any children are, you know,
            technically, because children can't, um,
            consent. So there's no such thing as a.

            They were actually children who were. Um,
            convinced by aid workers into performing
            sexual acts in exchange for food and

resources. And one of the aid workers was
my ex-fiancé. And one of them was my dad.

SIMONE makes a loud, involuntary, surprised noise.

SIMONE: Oh. My. God.

CARYS: I've never said that out loud before.

SIMONE: It's okay.

CARYS: I've been in therapy for six weeks and I've
not managed to actually. Sorry.

SIMONE: Don't be.

CARYS: I have no idea why I just told you that.

SIMONE: Carys. It's okay. It's not your fault.

* * *

SCENE THREE

9.53pm

The restaurant. JASON is waiting for GODFREY, alone with the donuts.

*He stares at them like an opponent. Gets very close, opens the box.
Begins, very slowly to choose one of the two remaining donuts and even
more slowly to remove it from the box. Then enter GODFREY, carrying
a larger box of donuts. There is something simultaneously gorgeous and
intimidating about him, it is difficult to place what. GODFREY's every
move is swanish, precise, effortless.*

GODFREY: Would you like a /donut

JASON: People shouldn't leave things here overnight
Hello Godfrey.

GODFREY: Oh don't worry about that. I leave them out for the rodents. Haha.

JASON: *(Not sure if he's joking.)* Oh. Haha?

GODFREY: I've got fresh ones here. Have one.

(JASON does.)

GODFREY: They're birch seed and raw cacao.

JASON: *(Chewing, with disappointment that verges on anguish.)* Lovely.

GODFREY: Sit down, Jason. Have a seat.

The two of them take opposite seats at a table, donuts in the middle. GODFREY takes out a hip flask from his inside pocket and pours them both a drink of whisky. It should feel very much like an awkward first date, GODFREY brimming with confidence and charisma, JASON trying very hard to seem relaxed to cover his sudden feeling of inadequacy.

GODFREY: Japanese. Very strong. Organic. Graham and I have it imported.

JASON: Mmm. That's good shit.

GODFREY: Indeed.

A pause while the two men sip and chew.

JASON: How was your…day?

GODFREY: Oh, you know.

A pause.

GODFREY: Are you married, Jason?

JASON: Am I – I'm not, no. I'm kind of seeing this chick, but like –

GODFREY:	Not married, you're not married, no. I was married at your age.
JASON:	I didn't know you were – how long have you been married for?
GODFREY:	Was married. Not anymore. Twenty-one years.
JASON:	Oh. Well. Twenty-one years, that's. A milestone.

GODFREY finishes his whisky, so JASON does, GODFREY pours them both another.

GODFREY:	My wife and I separated three years ago. Back when I first started practicing Buddhism. Well, we were on holiday together in Goa, one of these retreats, you know, my wife and I and Graham.
JASON:	Graham is your – ?
GODFREY:	Graham is my lover.

JASON is unsure what to say to this but wants to say something.

JASON:	How did you – meet – him?
GODFREY:	Well, we met out on the allotment one autumn, three harvests ago. He had grown the most tremendous tomatoes, I vividly remember seeing them for the first time. Heinous shades of scarlet and vermillion. Healthy streaks of lustful Tuscan orange.
	Well. At last Graham and I got talking. We went for some drinks. As it turned out we had much the same taste in everything – music, art, literature…we began to spend a lot of time together. I invited him to

Goa with us, which naturally made Janine
suspicious, and to cut a long story short,
we had three weeks of mountain trekking,
meditation and hideous rows. Very, very
ugly rows. The things that were said
between the walls of that Ashram…well, it's
shameful, Jason, utterly shameful from all
three of us.

JASON downs the last dregs of his whisky.

GODFREY: I used to store a lot of anger, in my lumbar.
Here. *(He places JASON's hand on his lumbar.)*
Vinyasa Flow has helped me tremendously
with that.

Janine and I filed for a divorce pretty much
as soon as we'd done baggage claim, and
Graham and I have been life-sharing ever
since.

*JASON is, for the first time in his entire life, utterly speechless.
A long pause, in which GODFREY is comfortable and JASON is
uncomfortable. Eventually –*

JASON: Was there like, a reason you wanted to have
a meeting or –

GODFREY: From next week onwards I'd like you to
manage the restaurant. Supervise. Whatever.
I've built this company up from nothing.
I've put Streatham on the map. We have
branches set to open in the new year:
Hoxton, Brixton, Copenhagen. But in terms
of right now, I would like to be able to
actually have a social life again, even if just
for a bit, and to spend time with Graham
and the dogs. I do think Simone would be

good at it, better than you even despite your confidence, but the thing is, I just can't trust a Gemini…with that sort of responsibility. Superficial, indecisive and unreliable, the lot of them. I'm sorry, but they are. Especially around this time of year.

JASON: Oh.

GODFREY: In other news, perhaps you'd like to come for dinner some time? You and Simone and…

JASON: Carys.

GODFREY: Carys. Graham is a performance artist, by trade, but he shows me up in the kitchen all the same. He makes the most fantastic Moussaka. Moist and tangy and fragrant. It's to die for.

JASON: …

GODFREY: Your hours will be the same, only I'll need you to close every night so that Simone can have a break. She's doing so much. In fact remind me, I must ask her to stop with the rodent poison. It's barbaric. And your wage will go up, of course, an extra one fifty an hour. Remember, loyalty goes a long way in this business, and it's always rewarded. How's the new girl getting on?

JASON: She's. Weird.

GODFREY: Well of course. She's a libra isn't she?

JASON: –

GODFREY: I've been feeling a bit weird myself recently. Maybe it's the blood moon.

EPILOGUE

10.18pm.

The staff room. SIMONE and CARYS are getting ready to leave work.

SIMONE: Hey! Carys, I have a quote for you. I follow this meme account on Instagram that does daily inspirational quotes and I have a quote for you.

CARYS: …

SIMONE: 'The state of just having lost something is the most enlightened state of being.'

CARYS: …thank you.

SIMONE: I think that's a really good thing. I'm all about enlightenment.

Listen, Carys, can I..? Um. You're gonna be okay. What happened to you was horrible, and completely not your fault and I think you feel a lot of guilt because you're a woman and you've –

CARYS: Sorry, argh, can we –

SIMONE: But you're a really cool, lovely person and you're gonna be okay –

CARYS: Why? No I'm not! Why am I going to be okay?

SIMONE: Because you've been through some shit, but now you can reclaim that shit, I'm not saying you have to be happy, not right now, I just don't want you to hate yourself. Sadness is, horrible, but you can *own* it, you know, you have a *pussy*, you're a *woman*, so own it –

CARYS: I don't know what you're – and not all women have – um –

SIMONE: I'm not talking about literal pussy! I'm not talking about vaginas!

I'm talking about whatever shit about yourself they made you hate, whatever shit you tried to disown. Hide about yourself. Whatever shit caused you to want to become invisible at any time. Pussy is – I'm talking anything female, trans, non binary, black, brown, queer, disabled, broke, inadequate, incorrect –

I'm talking anything they call minority, difference, anything that fills a diversity quota and makes you doubt your right to be there

I'm talking about reclaiming that

That's pussy.

Pussy is a state of mind, a state of soul, a state of enlightenment.

Pussy is zeitgeist

This is The Pussy Zeitgeist

We're caught in the middle of it

right now in this moment

And I'm not talking the commercial shit

Not the Girl power T-shirts

The feminist diamond necklaces

I mean wear that shit if you want that's cool
if that's you

But that's not what I'm talking about

And I'll say again I'm not talking about
vaginas

Vaginas are great, really great, but they're
only one optional dimension of the multi-
dimensional infinity that is pussy

Pussy has no gender and no lack thereof

Pussy does not know binary, does not notice
binary, has never even heard of binary

pussy transcends

everything

Pussy is the present, the past and the future

And we have to cling to it

I'm telling you now, babes, we have to cling
to it, because if we don't they'll take it and
sell it, which is why we've got to come back
hard and fast and loud and ugly and pissing
them off

Pussy is choosing who you don't mind
pissing off and knowing it's beautiful

No, not beautiful

Fuck beautiful.

POWERFUL.

powerful and influential and

able to make tears fall from hardened people and consciousnesses shift and movements start and

What a piece of work is pussy!

All Shakespeare ever wrote about was pussy!

It's our turn.

It can be whatever we want it to be

That's pussy

That can be your pussy

If you want it to be

Do you want it to be?

A long pause as they both return to reality.

CARYS: I don't know. That's. Um. A lot to take in.

SIMONE: Carys, I don't know if you know this but there's a blood moon tonight.

             A blood moon is really good for healing, and new beginnings, and rebalancing so I was thinking maybe it would be good for you with your therapy.

             I was going to go and watch it with this guy, but he doesn't want to come and he's trash anyway and I think I'd rather go with you. If you want to.

CARYS: ...I'd love to come.

SIMONE: Oh my gosh, really?

CARYS: Yeah.

END OF PLAY.